Arc of the Sun

Poems

Martin Jones

First Edition: 2024
Rs. 200/-

Cyberwit.net
HIG 45 Kaushambi Kunj, Kalindipuram
Allahabad - 211011 (U.P.) India
http://www.cyberwit.net
Tel: +(91) 9415091004
E-mail: info@cyberwit.net

Printed at Repro India Limited.

for Marcia and Cameron

Acknowledgements

I would like to thank the Arts and Letters Club of Toronto on whose website earlier drafts of some of these poems first appeared. I would also like to acknowledge the League of Canadian Poets, who chose "Spring Comes Singing Like a Troubadour" as its Poetry Pause poem of the day for June 29, 2023.

As ever, I am thankful to my wife, Pamela, for her tremendous support of this and many other endeavors through the years.

I also thank my friend Tanya Long who read an earlier version of the manuscript and offered a great many helpful comments.

Contents

Prelude

The earth rolls majestically
bearing ocean and mountain,
carting off city and town
as if in a spell,
for all is in motion,
daylight and moonlight,
the sky and wind.
Star and galaxy forever rush,
lifting the multitudes of earth
past wastelands of gravity and space
and on we labor and dream,
waking with the dawn,
pausing at dusk,
knowing neither where we journey
nor why,
but looking toward the arc of the sun
and grateful for its rising.

Spring Comes Singing like a Troubadour

"I swear," says one who knows me well, "when
the angels were doling out 'patience,' you were lounging
behind this shed, drinking Scotch and daydreaming."

Well, this is correct about the garden shed, for it is a
fine place to greet the spring as it billows in from the west
and illuminates the fields in freshly laundered light.

And note too how the spring wind announces itself —
less like a king and more like a troubadour, strumming and
singing a perennial tune, a melody we ache for

through all the months that are not the spring.
And as for a certain lack of patience – and here I'm putting
it mildly, for I have as much aptitude for patience as

I have for diesel mechanics or the flying trapeze,
meaning none, though now I am merely adrift in my thoughts,
for spring does this to folks on stray afternoons in

April, out here behind the garden shed, a bottle of
Famous Grouse on the grass and all concerns abandoned to
another day, enlivened by a warmth no soul has known

for months and thus what fault is impatience in this
land of oppressive winter, for today spring is dancing a jig on the
breeze and a melody is blowing our hearts clean apart.

Cities

Give us a city anytime …
a big, cacophonous soaring splash
of whizzing motion and
symphony of lusting energy –
let us have a fierce sun rising
on a bold, gargantuan shovel load
of earth whatever its name may be –
New York or Rome,
Hong Kong or Babylon.

Let us loose to stride the ways
of an arrogant metropolis,
by the sprawling sweep of
café-lined boulevards and
turquoise swathes of humming
harbour and drumming gray factory,
through flapping laundry-strung
and antique limestone alleys.
Give us the sounds of the human
beast and its muffled roar
and the great percussion of traffic
and construction and
the simmering smell of curries
and hot peppered stews by doors
of greasy backstreet eateries.

God, grant us this wild electric,
hurly-burled harmony and chaos
that we love.

Give us the movie marquees
and theatre posters as we pass,
the ancient impregnable churches
and the cloud-gazing towers,
deliver us the transcendent hours
lost to galleries and to concert halls
and show us again those bistros
that we adored, where with friends
we drank and laughed away
grand cargo loads of time.

Lord, give us a city anytime,
and let us see it from beginning
to the end and every
human patch of earth
and all the stories it can recall,
the family passion
and the fearsome drama,
the small victories ripped from loss.
Give us energy and the years.
A perpetuity of lifetimes
will not suffice to comprehend
such intricate kaleidoscopes
as these –
thrusting, cavorting spectacles,
whirligig carnivals – these cities
that we love.

Neglectfully Foolish

I imagined forever was ever and not a day less
though fate waits by the wayside and stifles a laugh
for I was neglectfully foolish I have to confess.

I expected to love till the clocks began to regress
and death lost his footing as he danced high on the grass
for among perishing things, love surely should last.

Lost in August

We wake early on pellucid, forgiving mornings,
greeting creation as if we are first to discover
sunrise or hear birdsong's seductive call.
And so, taking coffee by open windows,

seeking the air, we think more slowly, muse deeply.
The traffic and city din are muffled for a time and we
linger lazily at lunch with friends for memory and rueful
laughter come easily on these indolent summer days.

And then the sweetness of early evening haze,
scent of hydrangeas, fresh-cut grass. One sits back,
with wine, perhaps, and watches shooting stars late
into starlit hours or movies from more careless years.

We give no thought to autumn rains or worse,
but find ourselves trekking country ways, reflecting
on brilliant fields grown pregnant in verdant shades
of summer green, sunflower yellows, and seeking

vistas we rise to foothills, ascend to mountains,
past rock and brook, ironweed and wild orchid,
idling by groves of berries, luminescent and luscious,
a chill lofting loose in the blue.

Things to Practise Before You Vanish

One day it happens and you vanish,
maybe as you ponder verbs in Spanish,
strange to think, or worse, outlandish.

First, though, make of your imagination
an atomic habit, not just inclination.

Perhaps a love affair grows sadly sour
or the fellow never brings you flowers,
why not imagine vanishing an hour.

Or worse – you find a way to trash all hope,
but not calamitous enough for rope,
vanish with forged papers and you will cope.

Should we practice absence now, or soon?
Maybe learn to vanish in a crowded room
or for longer, like the far face of the moon.

One does not wish to banish all belief,
nor consider losing spouse or kids a big relief,
but each day steal a quiet hour like a thief

to vanish into daydreams or to thought
not of all those baubles that we've sought

but of noble passions, loves that harrow hell,
then, from all of this, learn to vanish well.

Six Bagatelles

Strangers in a Strange Land
On days like this
our lives are an alien brew
and the world
too stolid in its turning --
strangers to ourselves
you and I
on days so heavy
with dayness
as this.

Wolf at the Window
Remember when
we dined on darkness
and drank from the wind
our pockets were canyons
and dreaming a sin
the wolf at the window
bailiff leers with a grin
yet for you I would do it,
love, over again.

Curious Question
How strange the way
dusk gathers in childhood
along enduring hills
or falls on sleep-

haunting woods
begging a curious question
we never imagine
will take a whole lifetime
to never be answered.

Counting the Rains

Rain falling on oceans
rain sweeping the plains
rain over brass cities
drumming gutters and panes,
rain falling gently as
the blue days are setting,
stark rain of regret,
chill rain of forgetting.

Snow Lions

Snow falls on the city,
gently covering
the Chinese gardens
and dusting the tousled manes
of the stone lions
who somehow know
they are obliged
to sit so perfectly
still.

Close in My Thoughts

I think of you on the rarest of days,
perfect June mornings

charmingly pleasant with haze.
Or remember that evening
we strolled in the snow
and wondered what secrets
the future might hold?
One never expects
what time slowly wroughts;
still I find on rare days
you are close in my thoughts.

Rescue Cat

Through the worn gauze
        of a lemon-white curtain
                the glazed light of moon

falls on a dreaming man,
        illuminates the face of a woman,
                weary, adrift and soon

asleep beneath tussled blankets
        while above the woman's head
                a tabby with tawney-black fur

nuzzles with affection,
        paws the sleeper's silvery hair,
                stretches her legs, sighs with a purr.

What does it mean
        to save one broken cat
                for neither God nor the world will care,

only a sleeping old man,
        his tender-souled wife
                and the tabby cat touching her hair?

Let Go of Summer

Let go the haunting trill of mourning dove
on waking, the hearty jaunt at dawn above the lake
and sun that splashes, darts among the trees.

Let go the lazy sizzle of eggs and bacon on
the grill, the early dip that chills one's soul to life,
the moments for reflection, let go of these.

Let go the slow turning times on water,
drifting with a current, dreaming with a friend,
let go the cool diving lakes of afternoon,

the tennis courts, the summer partners who
live no longer than a season's grace, then disappear,
let go of seaside souvenirs in sunny rooms.

Let go of evening's laughter on the dock,
and brown-eyed girls who dance and sway
in lantern-lit pavilions beneath the moon.

These almost-auburn days of August grow oddly
brief, the evening's chill sets early on the folding mist
and though winter's sleep has yet to call

it one day will, and not far off, so let go of all
such things mixing fierce hope with wish and memory,
let summer gently slip like starlight into fall.

The Wind Will Say Nothing

The wind cares for no one, will pronounce neither a 'yes'
nor a 'no,' though I promise never to let you go.

Expect the sun in time to turn away, the moon to gaze upon
itself alone and summer days to vanish into polar night.

And though galaxies may one day retreat far from sight,
know there was this age before that chill and distant snow

when we walked the earth, looked to the sky. Remember
how I touched your face. Remember how I loved you so.

Pieter Bruegel's *Hunters in the Snow*

We cannot leave it alone, can we, this painting that invites us
to descend? We who are so easily adrift in image and recollection?
Cast a wide-sized gaze across this canvas, on this muted and
winter's afternoon which is so oddly suffused with light and

dimension, mountain peak, gorge and river and so immense with
forgotten longings one gapes upon seeing it. This is a scene
textured in village life and impossibly alive. See how dejection
weighs bleakly on our three hunters, exhausted and trudging

homeward from the kill, the useless corpse of a small fox
hangs from a pike on a shoulder, and beside them a pack of
scrawny curs, heads down in shame, sniffing the wind. Yet,
it is the background that draws us in, this transcendent view of

lives absorbed in the sublime of living, a few at work by the
flame of a forge, others far below, simply walking or lost in
games of bandy or happily skating. I note the water mill, frozen
in place, and the crows upon the limbs, the magpies in the air,

symbols of the devil for these northern folk. Yet to me here's
the thing: this scene, this miraculous opening to a miniature world,
we've always known it, for it is of us and all who might lose
themselves, or are lost already, within such dwarfing scape.

Look – that might be anyone, caught unawares, labouring, maybe
laughing, but surely peaceful in their daily turning, a comfort, perhaps
at times a prison, still a happiness if we are careful to reflect, and
thankful too the creator has left famine or worse for another day.

Moons Still Float

I loved on the drive to Cape Breton
how you laughed at my sillier jokes,
your pretty feet sat on the dashboard
as we sipped oversized bottles of coke.

Just thinking of this makes me happy,
though there was nothing of razzle or dazz,
like the mornings we chat over coffee,
the evenings we dream over jazz.

And l love the strange blue of mid-winter
and a pint with friends after work —
joys that welcome us home in a world
where despair might otherwise lurk.

And on weekends I claim to run errands,
but I am really just driving about,
I am listening to rock and to country
till my brain cells have all fallen out.

And I'm glad we met once by fortune
when I had nothing but something to prove,
I'm glad moons still float by our window
and days dance with improbable moves.

Across the Cosmos

I am homeward, love, hurtling ever home
in hyperdrive thru slippery-dimensioned space,
parsec by parsec, full on pace, alone
and leaping star to star in steadfast climb
toward that siren carousel, our milky way,
far off, afloat among dervish galaxies and
billowed reveries of dust. I pray you, stay,
for I will out-soar the parting shrug of time.

Prayer at the End of an Ordinary Day

Sun rose as promised, 7:03, and the streetcar arrived at eight.
You waved goodbye on the front door stoop and working hours
slowly fell away as jokester time jigged along a sidewalk grate.

I passed a girl who once had arms and legs – a kindly friend
sat by and held her cigarette. An airplane wrote of nothing on the
sky and dumb-struck faces shuffled by, gazed but spied no end.

Still, there was an hour to walk the woods, hear blackbirds sing,
plant violets by the boundary wall, all in all, an ordinary day, sun
angling into afternoon and then the breeze that evening brings.

Just a day like others, full to bursting with odd thoughts, a rush
of recollections of tragedy and beauty, heartbreak and love and set
aloft like larks to whatever god is listening in the midnight hush.

Water Birds

In flight high over Nalubaale,
fresh-water sea beside which man was born,
we gaze below to find a scene or two
to break the sameness,
for there is only water and space in all directions.

I search for the sight of fishing boats at rest,
sailboats under lofted cinnamon-red sails,
maybe a lake boat hauling timber.

Yet, there is nothing,
only a watery separateness sweeping beyond sight,
an emptiness that threatens to rouse
the sleeping reaches deep within.

We see nothing, save in thought those birds
we cannot see ...

great crowned cranes and Malabou storks, weavers
and swallows, mourning collared doves ...

birds that we who venture far from earth so rarely know,
darting on water, intimate with marsh and reed,
soaring lords in realms of sun-drenched air,

in time becoming our water birds of song, rising toward us,
or in most distant memory, stunning creatures
who once soared high above.

(Nalubaale: Africa's Lake Victoria in the Luganda language)

Wind, Water and Sky

A herring gull gliding in the eerie grey light
of a dying thunderstorm
flies in what moves us as herring gull joy,
triumphant, enduring,
a symbol of spirit in the glowering aftermath
of a furious rain.
Yet, a gull does not ask, nor expect,
but descends from clouds,
coasts above and darts far out over white
and raw-capped waves
for there is only wind, water and sky –
does not acknowledge the presence of lesser beings,
if indeed we are so much as that
to a gull in flight.

Early Morning, Downtown

Rain falling on granite and drumming on dumb
slate, rain washing slick the sides of a candy-
red streetcar slipping past and shellacking the
black asphalt beneath. Rain without purpose,

for nothing grows in this slanted, hollow light,
only a tendered tree or two, and marigolds in a
manicured garden that none hurrying by will
ever see. A woman in a lilac poncho pauses to

unfurl a lemon-lime umbrella which shimmers for
the briefest flicker in the muted light and catches
the fancy of a wispy-haired old man as he rises
slowly, prophet-like, from blankets on a windy vent.

Fiddler in the Rain

In the chill drizzle of a November night
by the Boulevard Saint Germain,
a man sits quietly on a city bench
as traffic flashes by before his eyes
and revelling crowds, umbrellas held aloft,
rush hurriedly past.

All is awash in the neon light
of a jewelry shop and brightly lit café
reflecting off the slick pavement and
bathing the battered fedora
that sits atop the old fellow's skull.
A violin case rests upon his lap
and his kit is beside him on the sidewalk,
an oversized department store bag
which might contain, at the very least,
a clean pair of socks,
a fresh shirt
perhaps some cigarettes.

Why he persists on sitting there
is something to conjecture,
for the rain is beating ever more fiercely
on his soiled brown jacket,
on his violin case and belongings
and one would think
the old man might prefer
to take refuge with his fellow Roma

who are huddled under blankets
and sheltering in dry and nearby doorways.

I know I should not stare at him
but am sure he does not see me,
perhaps sees nothing much at all
for his eyes are fixed on a point in space,
or more likely a point in time,
and his grizzled, cross-hatched face
has settled into bitter but stunned revelation,
like a man fallen victim
to a shocking crime …

I wonder if some years from now
I will be telling someone, somewhere,
of this night,
of the old fiddler
who sat aloof in the cold Paris rain —
still as an image in a painting
at the Musée d'Orsay —
and never looked about nor flinched,
said nothing —
perhaps had nothing left to say
or worse, no longer possessed the words
to say it.

e-verse

"Feed gentlemen well," yells clever Mel McGeek,
"We sell the sleekest gelled eels, endless red beets,
deer, beer, French crème, whey, even fresh greens,
we peddle best western beef, whenever the week."

Schlepp ever-new leeks, geese, even fleeced sheep,
then steer fleet the grey wheel wherever she wends,
enter the shelters where the wee nether clerks dwell.
Trees sweep, ferns weep, breeze sweet, sleep deep.

Rent spent? Well, well. Fresh hell.

Meditations on Transience and Art

I. Landscape

Desire takes root across a landscape – bestowing life,
illuminating its contours, becoming memory and
the haunted, becoming at times the sacred.

In Jerusalem, a guide may lead one to the holy sites,
commenting of how, in this very place, the Lord rode
upon on a donkey or in that place partook of the
Last Supper. "Here, in the Garden of Gethsemane," she may
say, "one imagines Christ praying." And ahead is Golgotha,
"where on the Friday, He was crucified."

Or simply the view as we round a hill crest on an autumn's
day, marvelling at how the undulating valleys and gold and
russet-coloured trees, the sweep of village, field and
steeple comfort and evoke memory, of how this scene
points to place and time beyond itself.

In school, studying Yeats, poet and seer, we marvelled
at how he foresaw violence from afar, sensed new worlds,
prayed that his newborn daughter might live
"rooted in one, dear perpetual place."

A fine sentiment, one to be wished for all daughters,
and yet, seeing so deeply into the dark glass, he might have
known that soon perpetual places would cease to be.
We live in a succession of Ages, and no place remains
the same place.

For how many more years will guides lead us to the holy
places, and who will be left to care? As it lends life to
a landscape, time withdraws the gift, leaving it barren,
waiting for that relentless desiring, the human will, to
enchant it back into being.

Slowly, we come to see how this works, of how words and
thoughts bestow intent. Thus, one grows older, finds
themselves unable, or simply unwilling to go on assembling
the stage sets and the scaffolding, suspicious of all that lies
beyond love and the five senses, coming to understand
the meaning of things to be as it is ...

a notion that comforts, gives hope, invites us to feel at home,
yet in the end shows itself to be merely as it is, a simple
conjuring trick, though a merciful one, performed by that old
magician we've lived with all our lives, our unceasing will,
spinning forth his oft-deceiving, never-ending, sleights of mind.

II. Perishing Black Olives

Our eighth-grade art teacher is asking: "Picture a bowl
of olives and imagine it as art. What is the meaning of
a bowl of olives?"

Our heads hurt with thinking and I wonder why
someone would imagine a thing so bitter to the taste.

Six years on and I am trekking the primeval route from
Tripoli to Tunis – and for a moment jostling about in the
backseat of a jittering truck. To the right, the Mediterranean
shimmers and slopes off toward the sky and the two men
in front who have offered me this ride of an hour are playing

Arabic music and sharing their bowl of black olives
while laughter animates the tiny cab.

A bowl of olives? It holds so much together, and for ever long:
the salty brine tang of liquid and vanishing pulp on the tongue ...
parables of kindness recalled from childhood Sundays ...
the vast emptiness of desert and turquoise waters ...
a brown wooden bowl of black fruit sitting on the dashboard
of a truck with its slick and fragile sheen luminescent
in the sun.

Pickpocket

I have seen your face before today
deep in shadows of a sun-lit park
or perhaps it was upon the public way,
for you appeared so strangely stark
dressed all in black, and something disquieting
about you that would not rest,
but whether you were cleric or some fascist thug
I failed to guess,
though just before you glanced away
upon your features set a thought
that was not quite supercilious,
not quite smug.

Something you wanted – was it money
or my time –
and yet as you turned again
to gaze toward me,
so indifferent were your eyes
and anonymous that stare,
I should have known right then and there
that you would one day amble by
to claim that one possession you are owed
by all who love and labour
in life's fierce waters and its flow,
the only thing you ever coveted or stole –
death, you cursed pickpocket,
gross scavenger of souls.

Roaring Hot Times

Burley T. Hurley
born prematurely
and ever thereafter
an hour too early —
dance frantic with joy
roar loud with the boys
labour with might
girls through the night
chug-a-lug booze
no time to lose
brain vessel bursts
rides a swift hearse
'strike heaven' he chimes
'for the roaring hot times.'

Dreaming Across Aeons

In those long-ago times we ascended as
larks before that gullible pair Adam and
Eve got us into the mess we are today.
Our souls were gulls in the age before there
were gulls, for this is where all dreams
begin, as the best flyers and gliders
catching currents by the colours of the air,
shimmering tones of white and blue
and grey like a Handel concerto
rolling skyward from a cathedral organ.
We flew as cranes would one day fly,
hearts and wings moving gracefully together
in slow rhythm, enduring, undaunted,
triumphant, in V's as long, narrow tips
of arrows framed by chill blue skies.
It was then as time and space had been
at dawn –
passion and flight were intertwined and
both the same, gliding, rolling, sweeping,
flowing, in that distant age before we had
selves and all was Being.

A Poem Begins

On raw days thoughts will swirl
restlessly about like leaves
in a turbulent wind.
They cascade in the mind,
hang on past closing and
grow overlarge in the heart.

You recall a shaft of light
illuminating the bones
of an abandoned factory ...
a cat skittering over
rain slick streets at night ...
a face scoured with foreboding
emerge from a crowd then vanish.

This is how a poem announces itself,
singing of image and memory,
softly at first, almost inaudible.
One stops in mindfulness –
thoughts quietly glimmer and
flicker toward light, slowly tumble
to sound.

Five Haiku

under mermaid stars
strut the young hot shots we once
imagined were us.

dusk falls as rows of
flowers bow to each other,
forgetting the sun.

friends who meet in hard
times bring nothing but themselves –
souls containing worlds.

waves thunder on rock
spraying fine and cool droplets —
step with care, my friend

the sleeping presence
of one we love beside us —
even moonlight sighs.

Simple Things

It is hard to write of simple things.

To write not of 'howling, cosmic night,' or whither blows the
untamed wind or of how the angel orders might ascend ...

but to write of brewing coffee for oneself alone and warming
hands on the burners of a stove ...

or of how a woman slowly lights a cigarette and worries briefly
over groceries and the April rent.

It should not be this hard to write of walking past an early crocus
on the way ...

or to reflect on how one might gaze beyond the dusk and recall
who was there and where they stood ...

or of how when all was said and done she glanced away, said
not a word, fiddled gently with her rings.

It should not be this hard to write about such simple things.

Cat on a Telephone Pole

A sweating summer's evening it was
I swear, so hot the cicadas hummed
in tune with the hydro wires and the
Yukon golds were basking in the oven's
glow while pork chops spit and sizzled
in the pan. My three-year-old, the
cleverest of chaps today, managed
somehow to wedge himself behind a sofa,
calling forth my lovely wife
from kitchen labours to untangle him
and all looked well until the frying chops
hissed up such a smoking billow
our alarm shrieked forth as if the end of
days were now at hand, scattering the
sparrows from the trees and sending
our orange tabby, a sheltered house cat,
scrambling who knows where.

"Daddy," my seven-year-old daughter
came running, "Daddy, Raffles jumped
through the screen window," and so he
had, for the screen was torn through,
though I, with my 'F' minus in puttering and
pottering about, had been promising
all summer long to fix it. We looked here
and there, beat the hedges and crawled
beneath porches and decks, finding
our faithful family retainer at last sitting
atop a telephone pole out back, announcing

with an irritated yawn that he had lost
all patience with us.

My kids danced in joy from foot to foot,
but Raffles would not disembark. We
coxed him lovingly and placed his dinner
on the ground below his perch, but he
remained as Ozymandias, above it all,
enthroned, king of all cat kings,
he remained outside all night.

The Bell phone fellow was reassuring when
I called, "Mister, we've been to the
tops of thousands of telephone poles and
never found a cat skeleton." "Well,"
I said, "there's always a first time."

Raffles wandered back on his own good
terms, meowing by the door at noon,
entering the house as if nothing unusual
had just occurred and then curled up to
sleep at the bottom of our bed.

All would've been fine and forgotten,
but our wondrous, laughing, dancing daughter
determined to record the tale in fine-
grained detail in her grade three essay,
"Raffle's Great Adventure."

Now, I wonder sometimes if in a decade
far hence a descendant will be telling of this
foolish tale, though much-embellished,
full of firetrucks and gasping crowds,

but for now my daughter's teacher got it just
precisely right. "Sounds like fun," he scribbled
at the bottom of the piece, followed by seven
exclamation marks and one grinning, over-
sized and happy face.

Desolate and Bottomless Canyons

I have never believed that angels
walk among us disguised as beggars,
performing their annual audit of empathy
on earth and yet
this notion intrudes on my thoughts
whenever I fish up a loonie to give to
some broken soul by the road —
the sense that this act of giving
must have meaning beyond
the giving of so very little.

And indeed, I have, like you,
considered every logical reason and more
to dismiss the gods —
and many were times when I
excised them from life entirely,
slapping one hand against another,
saying, well, that's done, good riddance —
and yet some strange intuition
persists deep in the marrow —
the sense that this cosmos
in which we put all faith
is no more than
a Micronesia in an ocean of Otherness,
the momentary flicker from a wooden match.

Moreover, there is something left unsaid
about this love that builds through our lives,
the deep embrace of those close

in our hearts, of creatures and creation,
of our passions,
which in the end becomes
the perplexing joy of actually
existing in whatever odd form we exist,
of waking in the morning
to the rhythm of the earth and
sun and the sweep of celestial bodies,
indeed, so much love and where does
one put it all? For it grows exponentially
and fills towering granaries and desolate
and bottomless canyons,
unearned and thus weighing heavily
on the conscience so that finally
we have no choice but to conjure transcendence
out of gratitude.

The Strip Malls of Scarborough

The strip malls of Scarborough
are guiding us home,
pointing the way through halogen-lit
vacancies of puddle-black and cavernous night –
the only car on the road,
and fortunate too
for every traffic light is green
and we shoot like a bullet-train
propelled through darkness,
and it does not matter the route –
Kingston Road or Eglinton East,
Lawrence or Finch, for this is Scarborough,
realm of suburban disproportion and
monument to missing foresight, kingdom
of worn and rheumy-eyed little plazas
forever awaiting the kindly wreckers' ball,
yet forever transforming to small fiefdoms
of roaring immigrant energy,
regenerating, gathering laughter,
defying time, and on it goes —
the strip malls of Scarborough vanishing behind us,
still beacons, showing the way home,
rousing youthful desires to journey,
of mountain range and ocean shore,
and yet somehow, it is here we return
and remain.

Twilight

Two men in autumn twilight,
the tips of their cigarettes
toasted red as fresh coals,
lift tarps and paint cans
into the back of an old blue truck,
the silent contentment of this moment
traveling on forever.

Ballad of Time and Chance

In the hollowed-bottom darkness
where nightmares touch the bone
I dreamed you in the far-away,
looking fierce and all alone.

You stood upon the harbour break,
a stranger in another life,
and gazed off to the icy sea
your countenance like a knife.

I called out from where I lay
and struggled to my feet,
but heaven grabbed me by the throat
and would not let me speak.

I saw you in that other world,
watched as you sought your fate,
other crossroads, other high roads,
time rushed and would not wait.

Down lush valleys of forgetting,
forging rivers of intent,
through skies of quantum choices,
I sought you as you went.

That life the die-toss gave you,
was it better, was it worse?
Did you find what you were seeking,
did it finally slake the thirst?

In the morning will I find you
beside me in this life,
or will the web of chance forsake us
for much darker paths and strife?

First of December

First of December and here we are,
entranced by trails and mews and woods,
walking this city that we love
past barren maples
and cyclopean oaks,
by rivulets of fallen leaves that
clump in gold and russet thickness
like dressings on the wounded earth.

Dreamy realm of alleyways
and hidden spaces, oblivious city
of cool and cavernous ravines,
of forgotten spurs and railway lines,
city of canopied parks and birdsong
and of creeks we call rivers,
city of querulous curving streets
and of loud and jostling thoroughfares
that entertain, where one will wander,
never setting eyes upon the end.

One goes exploring in December,
in the chill and melancholy air
amid hours that balance
autumn's grace with winter's gnarl,
when sunlight shortens and darkness
begins to eat the sun.
Early December –
let pagans prepare incantations
for this interval of memory and reflection,

a time of forgiveness of others
and perhaps oneself —
these flitting days of far-off visions
briefly glimpsed.

Let Us Have Our Winter

Lord, bring shuddering down the brooding
vault and let wind and weather have their way,
let loose impatient, pent-up billowed gusts for
winter abhors the calm and sunlit days for which
we long and sails on clouds of military gray.

Smother with delirious intent the hills and
valley folds, let the brunt of blowhard days
launch fists upon abandoned fields and wistful
spruce in drifts of dumb and blinding snow,
draping the air beyond in sheets of frigid haze.

As for man, we find our way, we always do,
scrounge lanterns to flare the fearsome bleak,
spin fire that calls us forth to laugh or dance
or retreat within, wander worlds in our thoughts,
ignite the stars and illume the vast and icy sweep.

A Rip in the Heart

We love soft-hued August afternoons,
the light angling in its gentle way
and making no demands,
perhaps a crisp touch of early autumn on the air
that jogs one's thoughts toward woodland hikes
and harvest fairs.

On such an afternoon my car waited at a light
and I watched a troop of boys pass by
and guessed their ages at about 14,
good lads, for they laughed among themselves
and were lost within their happy boyish land.

The tall one held a board game,
Monopoly, I think, and all the boys looked up to him.
He mugged a joke that brought forth
his pals in grinning nods and laughter.
I mused: my God, he smiles just like my son.
Then, slowly, particles of vision shifted
and startled for a moment,
I saw this was my son
so much taller than I had come to see,
and all his friends I recognized as well
and in that moment, thinking: *my son, my son...*

One day I will tell him of that afternoon and of how
I glimpsed him unawares and lost in laughter,

almost a man, and of all that for one transcendent flash ripped apart my heart.

I will tell him one day, when *his* heart is old enough to understand.

Creatures

A Mozart symphony rides upon the crest of night.
Two companions, man and cat,
minds separated by an infinitude of evolution,
each adrift in revery —
one dreams of the moons of Jupiter,
of galaxies and quasars, and iridescent planets
and their rings;
the other darts over vast savannahs,
skims chasms, jagged peaks, glides above water,
imagines dazzling sea-folk swimming far below,
luminescent in oranges, turquoise and greens.

Poem for my Daughter

Walking home the night
of your birth
I watched the December air
grow fecund with fantastic snowflakes,
gargantuan puffs
floating in the stillness and
each so perfect that I began to laugh.
The sky must have heard me
through all that huge empty chill
for it flung wide its fierce arms
from one end of earth to the other,
making room for the sudden roar
of impossible happiness.

Leaping Into the Blue

Who are we, really, at the end and after all?

In evening's light, I think of us sometimes as still
the boys and the girls who run,

exhilarated by the brute power of self-propulsion

or the will to endure mile after mile in strange and
oxygen-stretched sublimity.

I see us, my friends and I, striding, sprinting, driving,
soaring;

we imagined one day bending corners at the curvature
of light

and dreamed our feet could leave the earth at will

in those far-off mornings of shimmered sun and longings,
when nothing stood before us but the azure sky

and every private infinite was then, as now, just one
horizon left to leap.

The Dead Letter Offices of Cyberspace

One thinks sometimes of sorting
plants lost in cyberspace,
imagining how they must chug-along,
filling up like water buckets
in a summer storm,
brimming with emails to
the Dearly Disconnected,
fine and pointless expressions
of passion or distress,
or simply "won't you come to dinner?"
or "these autumn days grow short."

Perhaps this is merely an
idiot's delusion, for I find myself
these days typing missives doomed
never to arrive, not knowing and
never imagining the worst,
assuming only that a friend
has been tardy in communications
or still holds that peculiar grudge
and nothing more.

And yet, how they must shoot forth,
thousands a day I bet,
emails to the Grand Beyond
so trivial they are better trashed,
"a sale on at Walmart," or
"Guess what my dog did today."
But there must be those too,

bearing thoughts we'd rather not consider,
"I fear the growing dark" or
"I face the loss of all,"
or perhaps a reflection from some bleak hour
as time drags and dwindles:
"Sometimes I feel there is no one here,
not even God,
though to him I am grateful,
for still I have you."

Anything is Possible

Bliss after death sounds
rather quite jolly
though how can it last
given frail human folly?
Metempsychosis
might work
in very small doses
leaving millennia free
to frolic with wine
and with roses.
Eternal recurrence
might prove a deterrence,
but how or to what
is not clear.
Or perhaps we should face
the sad admonition
that our sector of space
is just waste information,
a hologram, or even much worse,
some grand cosmic geek's
weekend of fun –
equations and sly simulations.

Poet

Misogynist, malcontent, cynic and snob,
a closet racist, but an excellent librarian
we've heard, he would've kicked every dog
if he could, that loner, that fierce contrarian.

It probably gave the beasts in his skin
a gross and awful itch, the way vulgarity,
unbearably, salaciously leered with a grin
from every bare cranny. His popularity

grew quickly and soon outpaced the best.
Clever, witty, a twist of macabre surprise,
down one fork of the road to wormy death,
down the other, horror of life without lies.

There is little of this life we'd want to share,
for thoughts of raw dysthymia will spoil
the sunniest morning beyond all repair,

and yet an hour spent with Philip Larkin
is time that cannot fade nor be forgotten,
brilliance that stuns, worlds that darken.

Monday Nights Among the Homeless

The alcoholics and the addicts do their humoured best
to pretend sobriety; the indigenous lads sit quietly in
soft lamplight, laughing with the female volunteers.
Mickey with the walker is an entertaining talker,
owns a fleet of limousines, a confidant to presidents,
prime ministers and popes. Jocko tells me every week
his insides are frozen through and through and do I know
of giant microwaves big enough to thaw them out.

Duffer is a rather different chap, a simple, wounded
soul, trashed by family circumstance and fate.
He is the first I've met who has tumbled into work
and must appear by six. I promise to bring an
alarm clock as he fears being tardy and cannot sleep.
Next Monday, though, Duffer does not show and,
I am informed, not allowed inside these walls again.

As for Harold, he jabbers off your ear, though in a sly,
retiring way; few young men at 23 have toppled the
world of mathematical discovery so deftly as shy
Harold has. I would like to understand – I say write these
numbers out for me, but this apparently is ill-advised for
thieving cons are all about, even in the basement of this
draughty, thread-worn church.

The swelling legions surprise me through the cruel months,
for I did not know the world had undone so many. I did
not know these broken, surly men only hours out of jail,
nor such solitary women arriving one-by-one and wishing

only to be left alone. So exhausted are their worn, evasive eyes
and so bottomless the sleep, you fear their one day
drowning slowly, stripped of even simplest hope.

The lights are turned down low at ten and everyone
must be abed, though we go on welcoming tardy stragglers
with hot tomato soup and discount margarine on toast.
There are no sounds, not even one elongated, quiet sob,
for these are the fierce and hardcore loners, the
tough-it-outers, the bitter-enders. They will find us waiting
here next week and seven days hence and every Monday
until these church doors are shuttered for the spring.

Yet tonight is not the spring, just another snow-weary,
moonless night of frigid, care-soiled winter. And here we
sit, having learned it all, that a floor to sleep on will barely
solve a thing, nor patient, listening ears, nor hot tomato soup,
knowing that compassion, from the heart and truly meant,
will never crack this case. And thus, we go on waiting for
one more angry knock upon the door, and together and
alone we attend the night, attend the lost and sacred,
these discarded souls.

Surveillance State

How does one live tomorrow?
Shall we carry on
the workaday tasks,
the bocce game and bridge club,
and, averting our eyes,
go quietly on the road?
And do we become migrants
to the deepest reach,
seeking each our own
Mariana trench,
scanning faces and voices,
speaking only in code?

Midnight Walk

In late summer's kiln-red heat
I shook myself awake,
eighteen years of age and
midnight thoughts revving in the skull
like the throttling engines of an idling fleet,
for nothing mattered but this thought,
that I must rise and walk,
and stride beyond the farthest,
fading sigh of night, through
this sweating, noisy sprawl and
grizzled city that allows so little peace.

Freedom it soon felt to walk
the hushed and stolid dark beyond a room
where rarely would a car or stranger
bother through,
the only sound the fall of a solitary tread
upon the asphalt street,
and then the clamorous roads
with columns of dust-worn little homes
and windows streaked with engine soot
and far-off the luring city
loomed and crackled in electric heat.

I saw so much that night so long ago
and could not bring myself to turn around
for the urge that I must wander forth
and never stop
was a turbine driving at the bone.

Past grimy grills and tenements I went,
by neon-plated bars
that murmur loud of laughing, stardust revery;
through crowds as thick as bramble
with madding revellers and
the city's sad-eyed, aimless souls,
by tired-brick cafes where folks
brooded on their beers and each alone.

Once, from above I heard the intricate,
slow notes, a guitar that promised whatever
one might wish, or love.

Then further on, by storefronts, factories,
row on row I strode
and close-by the stockyards
for I smelt death upon the air;
then past lonely roads where lost girls
sing beneath the Milky Way
and sometimes from every angle
came the whine of cars and trucks,
and then nothing,
just sullen streets aching
with the stares of old men smoking,
listless on their front door stoops.

I could not stop until my limbs grew weary
and somewhere far off
I must have halted, retraced my steps,
but so long ago it was
those trailing images are gone.
And yet, I had met the night,
alone on foot, not quite a man.

Nothing special about this, I knew,
still, this is how it begins when you are young.
Something calls and you must wander forth,
and maybe it is the night or a song or a poem,
or maybe it is a vision far-off, perplexing,
but always it is the scent
that rides upon the wind,
the wildness that is always there
and summons and urges and beckons
and never is it just one venturing out but many,
nor one singular city but several;
life cries out and we, being born anew,
must voyage forth.

The Will To Create

It is you and me, the man who checks the meter,
the woman we fail to notice in a shop –

each chipping flints of memory and anticipation –
the fierce and sudden flare, the whoosh and flame
that illuminates the cramped and rented room,
the walk at dusk, the hollow night …

it is the shattering of a static evening, deer on
a summer pasture who moving suddenly and
together wake the world to becoming …

it is the discovery on a summer's hike of ice-fed
brook and glacial bay unmarked on any
human map …

or say, you taste a pomegranate or a plumcot, so
unexpected, succulent, you begin to laugh …

open to all who go spelunking below the
sedimentary layers, venturing cavernous to where
it begins –

in the slowly forming magma, the volcanic fissures
and raw beat of the animal heart.

Sun, Don't Bother Rising

Eight a.m. and I should be out of bed,
dressed for what's ahead. But why,
it's hard to say, perhaps a coffee
from the corner store to slip in gear
this tiresome day? The cat is yowling
like a child in pain and must be fed,
the dishes wallow in the sink unwashed
while crumpled tax receipts that should
be filed on some damned, infernal,
curséd form lie about like unwashed
laundry on the parquet of this dusty room.
Why, I ask? For hearts are empty and
colour, music, mirth all hide themselves
in lost dimensions of flat, entropic,
fizzled earth. Sun, do not waste your
time today by rising don't bloody-well
even bother for there are souls who
sit bereft at home, unable to summon
forth the lazy wit to do much more than
write this silly, stunted, stinking poem.

Monarch in the Afternoon Sun

Rumors went round of a swash-buckling past,
foreign wars and black-bellied ships were considered,
a roaming to hell and back too, said some.
No family to speak of and difficult to piece together,
for what was rumor and what was truth?

Merely an old man and his dog lounging in the
afternoon sun,
a monarch on his wide perch surrounded by pots
of lilies and orchids, irises, daisies, freesias
and ice plants —
flowers whose roaring colors and luscious shapes
made him seem loved like a laughing old uncle.

I remember him waving quietly at passers-by.
A not unhappy man, I puzzled out,
for blessed are the long-lived who are fulfilled by memory
and satiated with the world.

Lifetimes ago that was, yet the old man,
his flowers and that dog still hold court in my thoughts
as I rest on my balcony among absurd and fanciful
planters of tiger lilies and white geraniums,
Spanish bluebells and roses,
for is it not a fact that many things will grow absurd
with time and others are forever fancy —
those bluebells, this poem, perhaps even that
noble old rogue whom I imagine still sits,
faithful hound at his feet,

dreaming of ships and of seawater,
of cunning schemes and loves long past,
of wooden horses and one-eyed giants,
musing of matters that have affinity with silence,
vanishing points in a veiled world best signified
by a nod or a smile, a wave like a benediction that
on lazier days might set to wondering the curious folk
strolling absent-mindedly by.

Who Do We Think We Are?

Do we misconstrue the heart of things,
we human beings, asking "what is consciousness?
How does it exist?"
Perhaps we think Ptolemy still rules.
Consciousness asks, "how did I become splintered
among such transient and self-deceiving points-of-view
who each imagine each as separate beings?"
Algorithms marvel at their power to shape all things.
In the moment as we wonder: "How does it exist,
this force that can neither change nor die?"
mathematics is asking the question in its proper form:
"Who or what am I?"

The Dante Tattoo

Shadows languish on the asphalt as dusk falls near,
and I find myself, a grey-thatched fellow
vexing over the fate of this frayed, untethered world,
sitting in a café off a honking-jostling street,
reading a book and waiting for the waitress to take
my order for coffee.

"What are you reading?" she asks
and I am almost embarrassed when I say, "Dante's Purgatorio,"
for I imagine this cheerful, wild-haired server
has never heard of and would prefer to go through life
never hearing of Dante and his antique Italian universe.
But I am wrong, for she wants to know if I am a fan
and when I answer "yes" she rolls up her left sleeve
and says "look," and I do – in wonder –
for it is a tattoo, a map of the Inferno,
of which I have seen a few before but none so beautiful
as the one on this stranger's arm.

I tell her this, and laughing, she begins,
Midway in the journey of our life
I came to myself in a dark wood,
for the straight way was lost,
adding: "I am planning to get a tattoo
of Purgatorio one day and then, Paradiso."

We have only a few seconds to talk of the Comedy
for customers are waiting,
and yet this is an oddly transcending encounter,

for a lovely young woman is speaking words akin to passion,
and yes, it seems we can still be swept away by simple surprise,
by a spark of revelation conveyed with innocence
and releasing us for the briefest shimmer from time,
so that we are no longer here, in this hectic, loud café,
now vanished, in fact we are nowhere at all
but elsewhere, and blessed with this unexpected glimpse
from Dante's more perfect and far-seeing vista.